Read and Remember

Individual and Group Activities
for Fiction and Nonfiction Reading

AUTHORS

Mandy Lohman
and
Erin Richardson

Carson-Dellosa Publishing Company, Inc.
Greensboro, North Carolina

DEDICATION

This series is dedicated to Chris Lohman and Kevin Richardson for their continued support and encouragement throughout this project.

Credits

Editor
Tara Poitras

Layout Design
Jon Nawrocik

Illustrations
Bill Neville

Cover Design
Peggy Jackson

Table of Contents

Introduction

Help students read **and** remember! The creative activities in this book were designed to improve students' reading comprehension skills—by addressing one story element at a time.

To help students focus on each story detail, activities are divided into four sections: Character, Setting, Plot, and Overall Story.

Activities for both fiction and nonfiction selections are included in each section. The activities can be completed by individual students, with partners, or by small groups. A quick visual reference is included at the bottom of each page to help teachers and students choose an appropriate activity. See the examples to the left.

Teachers can make packets of various activities for each student. Or, the activities can be used in a reading center, where students choose an activity to complete after they have read a fiction or nonfiction selection. During reading-group time, teachers can work with a small group of students to complete an activity. Advanced students that need to be challenged with independent work will also benefit from completing these activities.

Activity instructions ("What You Do") address the student. They can be photocopied for students to read themselves, or the teacher can give verbal instructions. A materials list ("What You Need") is included for each activity. Items are listed in the order students will use them. Some activities also include "Supplies You Could Use," a list of additional materials students might use to complete an activity.

Most activities include a "Note to the Teacher." This section includes any specific directions for the teacher, plus options for completing the activity.

FICTION ☺

This individual activity (☺) can be used with a fiction selection.

FICTION & NONFICTION ☺ ☺

This small-group or partner activity (☺☺) can be used with a fiction or nonfiction selection.

Master List of Materials

What You Need:

brads (2)
butcher paper (optional)
card stock (optional)
chalk
colored pencils
construction paper (assorted colors, including blue, brown, white)
contact paper (white and clear, optional)
tissue paper (assorted colors, optional)
crayons
envelope
glue
hole punch
markers
pencil
ribbon
scissors
stapler
tape
tissue box (square)
yarn

Supplies You Could Use:

poster board

CHARACTER KITE

What You Need:

pencil

Character Kite Template

scissors

crayons, markers

3 kite streamers

stapler

What You Do:

1. Make and display a kite about a character from a book you have read.

2. Write the book title, author's name, and your name on the Character Kite Template.

3. Cut out the kite.

4. On the back of the kite, draw and color a picture of the character.

5. Write one sentence about the character on each streamer. Staple the streamers to the bottom of your kite.

Notes to the Teacher:

- Cut 12" x 18" sheets of colored construction paper into 2" x 18" strips for kite streamers.

- You can copy the template on card stock for extra durability.

- Attach yarn to the tops of the kites to make a hanging display.

Character Kite Template

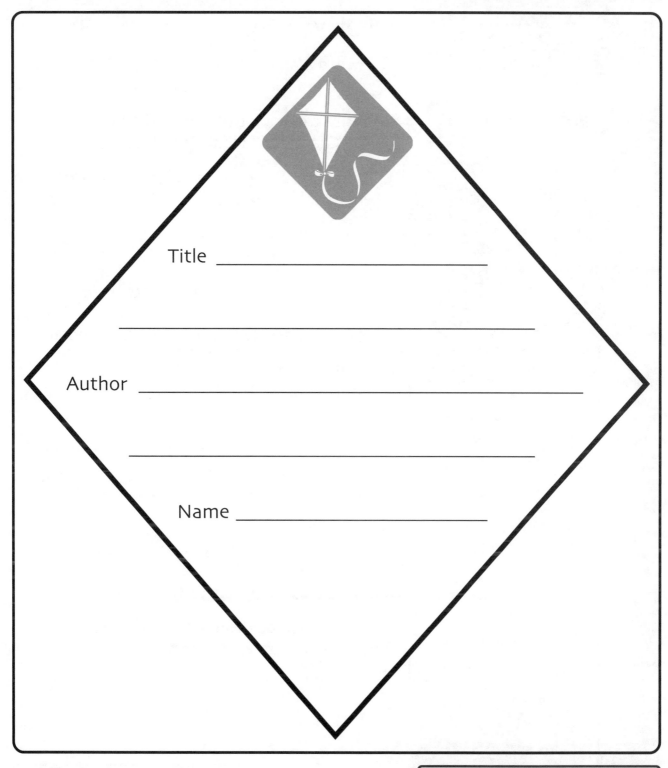

Title _____

_____

Author _____

_____

Name _____

CHARACTER MEDAL

What You need:

CHARACTER MEDAL
TEMPLATE

PENCIL

MARKERS, CRAYONS,
COLORED PENCILS

SCISSORS

GLUE

HOLE PUNCH

RIBBON OR YARN

CHARACTER MEDAL
ACTIVITY SHEET

What You Do:

1. Award a medal to a character from a book you have read.

2. Write the book title and author's name on the Character Medal Template.

3. Draw and color a picture of the character on the blank medal.

4. Cut out both medals and glue them together (back-to-back).

5. Punch a hole in the top of the medal and tie a piece of ribbon or yarn through the hole to form the necklace portion of the medal.

6. Write the book title, author's name, and your name on the Character Medal Activity Sheet.

7. Write three sentences on the activity sheet to explain why you like the character and why you gave him the medal.

Notes to the Teacher:

- If desired, you can hold an awards ceremony for students to show the medals and read their activity sheets to the class.

- Medals can be displayed on a bulletin board beside the activity sheets.

Character Medal Template

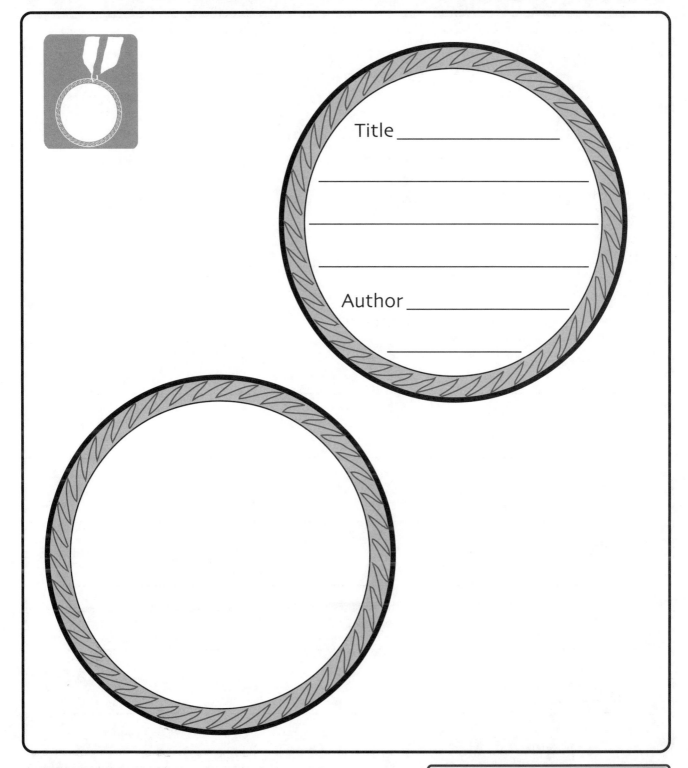

Title _____

_____

_____

Author _____

_____

Character Medal Activity Sheet

Your name _____

Title _____

Author _____

Character's name _____

I gave this character a medal because _____

_____

_____

_____

_____

_____

_____

Mosaic

What You Do:

1. Make a mosaic of a character from a book you have read.

2. Draw an outline of the character on the Mosaic Template.

3. Cut up small pieces of construction or tissue paper and glue them inside the outline. Use different colors of paper to make your mosaic colorful.

4. Write the character's name under the mosaic.

5. Write the book title, author's name, and your name on the Mosaic Activity Sheet. Then, write three or four sentences that tell about the character.

6. Glue the activity sheet to the back of your mosaic.

Note to the Teacher:
If desired, you could cut up pieces of colored construction paper and tissue paper beforehand and keep them in a box for students to use.

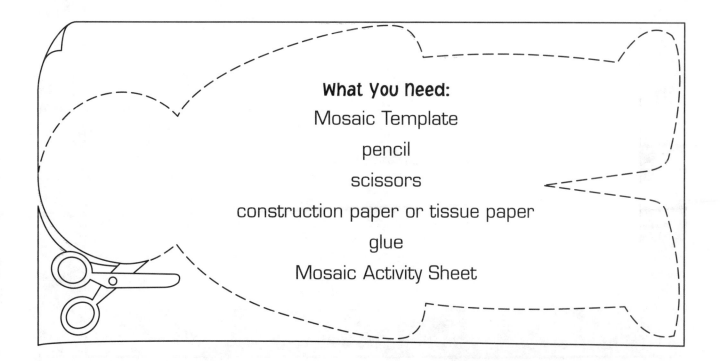

What You Need:

Mosaic Template

pencil

scissors

construction paper or tissue paper

glue

Mosaic Activity Sheet

Mosaic Template

Mosaic Activity Sheet

M

Name _____

Title _____

Author _____

Character description _____

_____

_____

_____

_____

_____

_____

Character Description

What You Do:

1. Describe a character from a book you and your partner have read.

2. Write the character's name on the Description Activity Sheet.

3. Talk with your partner about what the character looks like. On the three lines below the character's name, write three words or phrases that tell how the character looks.

4. Write a sentence that tells something about the character on the last two lines.

   For example, here is a description of Little Red Riding Hood:

   > Little Red Riding Hood
   >   little girl
   >   blond hair
   >   red cape
   > Little Red Riding Hood was brave.

5. Draw and color a picture of the character in the space above the sentence.

6. Write the book title, author's name, your name, and your partner's name on the back of the activity sheet.

Note to the Teacher:
Assign students to read a book with a partner.

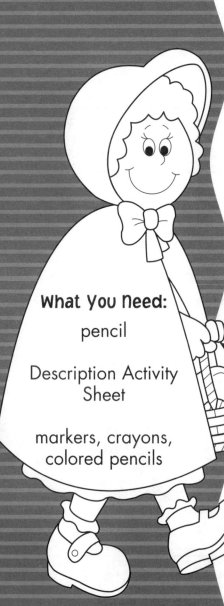

What You Need:

pencil

Description Activity Sheet

markers, crayons, colored pencils

Description Activity Sheet

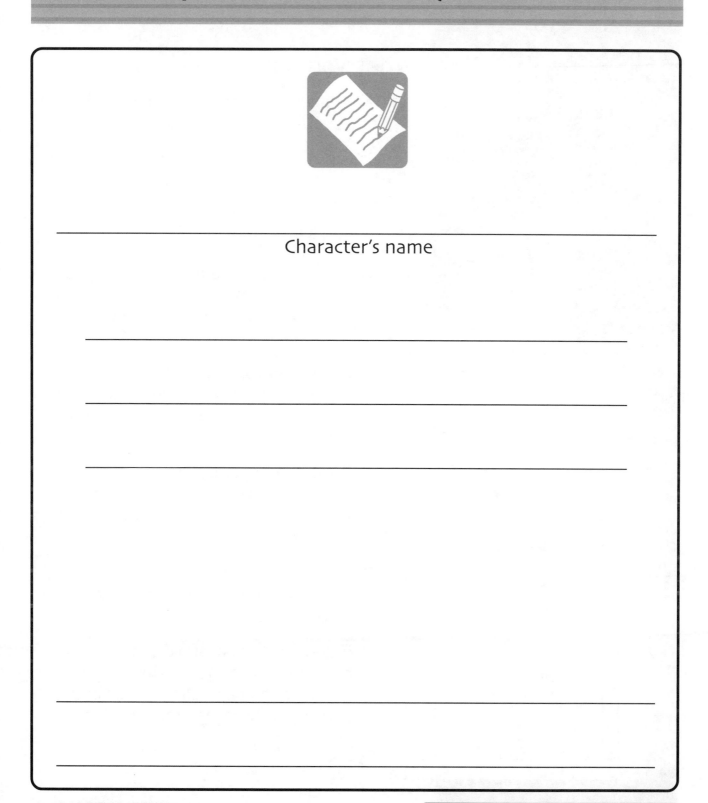

Character's name

FINGER PUPPETS

What You Do:

1. Make finger puppets of the characters from a book your group has read.

2. With your group, draw and color a picture of each character on the Finger Puppets Template.

3. Cut out each puppet.

4. Write the book title, author's name, your name, and the names of the classmates in your group on the Finger Puppets Activity Sheet.

5. Write the characters' names on the activity sheet. Then, write one or two sentences that tell about each character. Use the back of the sheet if needed.

6. Wrap the finger puppets around your fingers and tape them to fit. Use the activity sheet to describe the characters to the rest of the class.

Notes to the Teacher:

• Assign students to small groups to read a book together.

• If desired, each group can draw and color a background for their puppets on construction paper. Students can then perform a short play for the class.

What You Need:

Finger Puppets Template

pencil

crayons

scissors

Finger Puppets Activity Sheet

tape

Finger Puppets Template

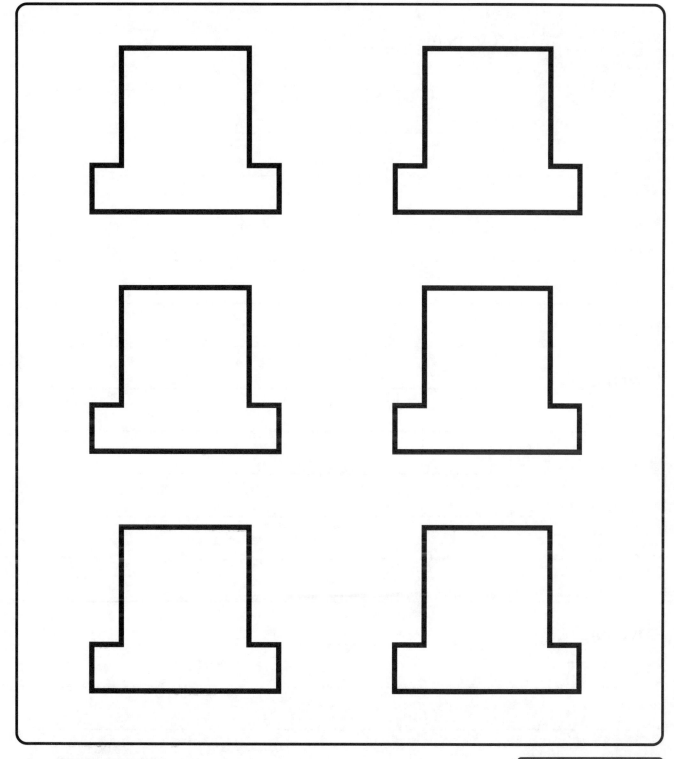

Finger Puppets Activity Sheet

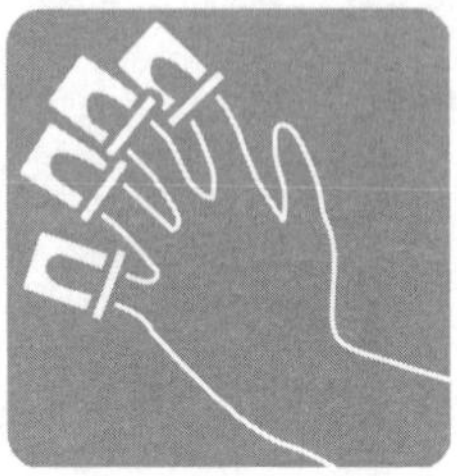

Your names _____

_____

Title _____

Author _____

Characters

Name _____

_____

_____

Name _____

_____

_____

Name _____

_____

_____

Name _____

_____

_____

Setting Quilt

What You Do:

1. Create a quilt to display the setting of a chapter book your group has read.

2. With your group, decide on the places from each chapter you want to include. Draw and color one place on each quilt section on the Quilt Templates. Write your name and the names of the classmates in your group on the bottom.

3. Write the book title and author's name on the last quilt section. This will be the center of your quilt.

4. Cut out the pieces and staple them to a bulletin board to form the quilt. Or, glue them to a piece of poster board.

Notes to the Teacher:

- Assign students to small groups to read a book together.

- Each group can make its own quilt. Or, if the class has read the same book, groups can combine their pieces to make a class quilt.

- Make enough copies of template #1 so groups have at least nine sections to make their quilts.

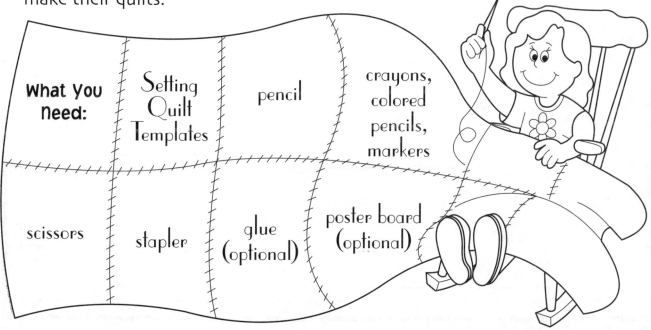

What You need: Setting Quilt Templates · pencil · crayons, colored pencils, markers · scissors · stapler · glue (optional) · poster board (optional)

Setting Quilt Template #1

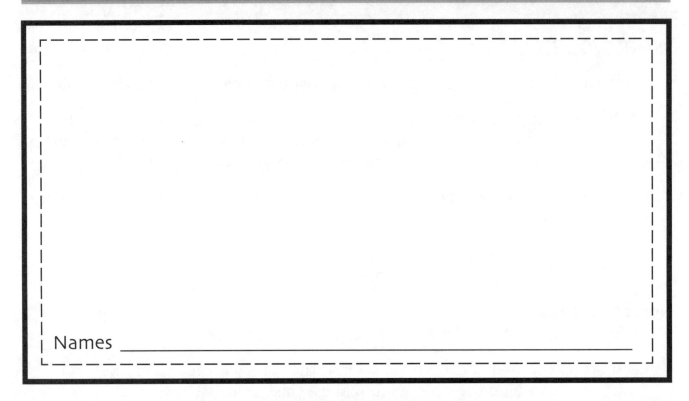

Names _____

Names _____

Setting Quilt Template #2

Names _____

Title

_____

_____

Author

_____

JIGSAW PUZZLE

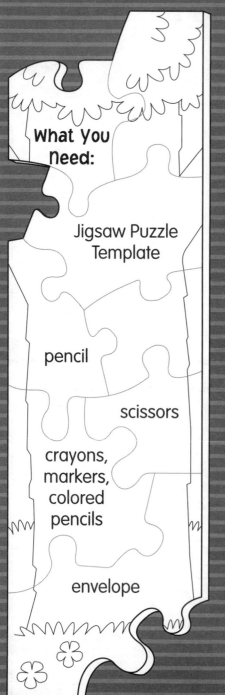

What You Need:

Jigsaw Puzzle Template

pencil

scissors

crayons, markers, colored pencils

envelope

What You Do:

1. Make a jigsaw puzzle of the setting of a book you have read.

2. Write the book title, author's name, and your name on the Jigsaw Puzzle Template.

3. Write three or four sentences that describe the setting.

4. Draw and color a picture of the setting on the back of the template. Your picture should take up almost the entire page.

5. Give the template to your teacher when you have completed it.

6. When your teacher gives your template back, cut the picture apart on the heavy black lines to make the puzzle.

7. Practice putting your jigsaw puzzle together.

8. Put the puzzle pieces in an envelope. Write the book title, author's name, and your name on the envelope.

Note to the Teacher:
Laminate students' pictures and draw lines on each with a permanent black marker to make eight puzzle pieces. You can also copy the templates on card stock or cover them with clear contact paper if a laminator is not available.

Jigsaw Puzzle Template

Name _____

Title _____

_____

Author _____

Setting description _____

_____

_____

_____

_____

_____

Book Train

What You Need:
Train Templates

pencil

crayons, markers, colored pencils

scissors

2 brads

What You Do:

1. Make a book train to show off the setting of a book you have read.

2. Write the book title, author's name, and your name on Book Train Template #1. Color the train engine.

3. On template #2, draw and color a picture of the setting on the boxcar. Color the rest of the boxcar.

4. Write three sentences on the caboose (on template #3) that tell about the setting. Color the rest of the caboose.

5. Cut out the engine, boxcar, and caboose.

6. Use brads to attach the three train cars together.

Note to the Teacher:
The trains can be displayed on a bulletin board for the class to read.

Train Template #1 (Engine)

Title _____

Author _____

Name _____

Train Template #2 (Boxcar)

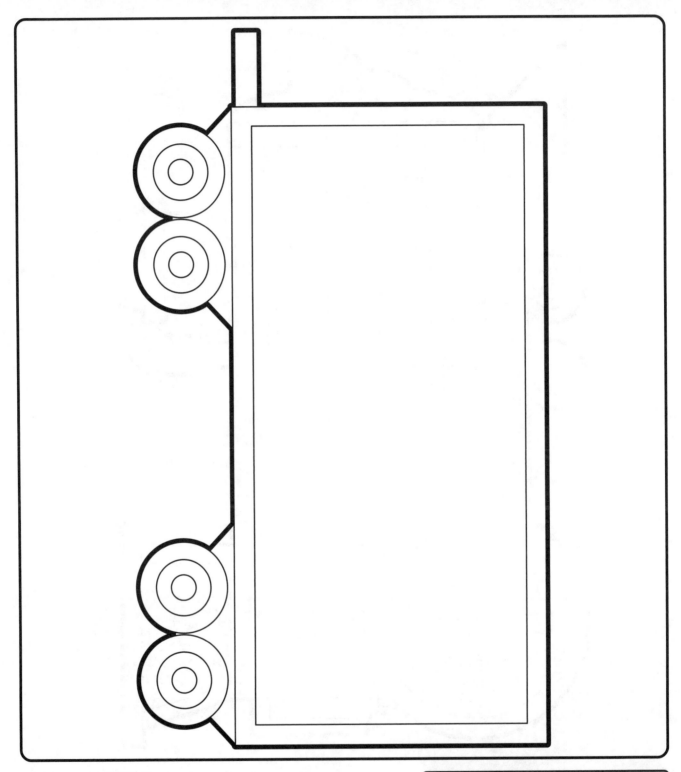

Train Template #3 (Caboose)

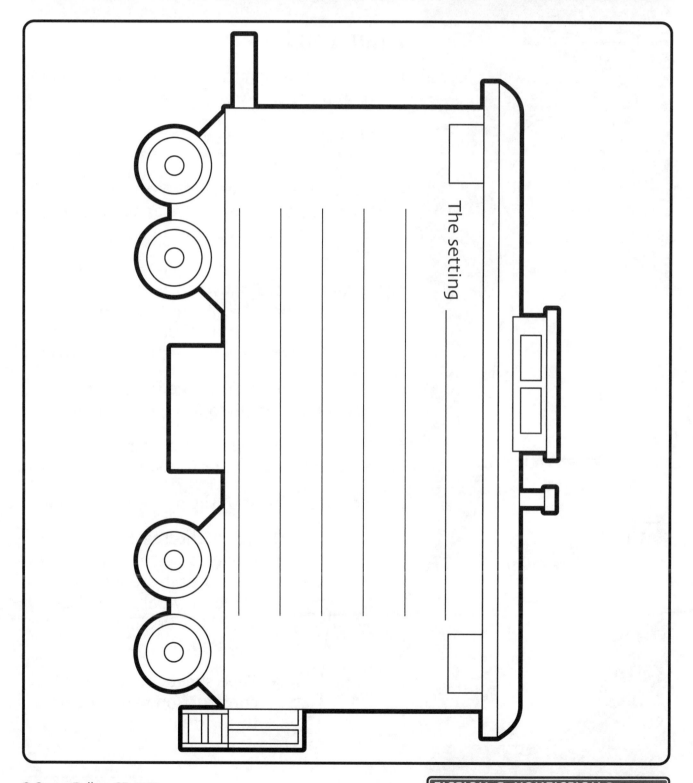

The setting _____

SNOWMAN STORY MAP

What You Do:

1. Build a snowman to show the plot of a book you have read.

2. Write the book title, author's name, and your name on Story Map Template #1.

3. Gather three "snowballs" (template #2). Write two or three sentences about the beginning of the book on the "Beginning" snowball.

4. On the "Middle" snowball, write two or three sentences about the middle of the book. Write two or three sentences about the end of the book on the "End" snowball.

5. Cut out the pieces and glue them to blue construction paper to form a snowman.

6. Make arms out of brown construction paper and glue them to your snowman.

7. Decorate the rest of the picture with chalk.

What You Need:

pencil

Story Map Templates

scissors

blue construction paper

glue

brown construction paper

chalk

Notes to the Teacher:

- Make copies of template #2 so that each student has three snowballs. Label the snowballs Beginning, Middle, and End.

- Tape sheets of 12" x 18" blue construction paper together to form 12" x 36" sheets.

Story Map Template #1

Title _____

_____

_____

Author _____

_____

Name _____

Story Map Template #2

MINI-BOOK

What You Do:

1. Make a mini-book to display the plot of a book your group has read.

2. Write the book title, author's name, your name, and the names of the classmates in your group on Mini-Book Template #1.

3. Work together as a group to draw and color a picture on template #1 about an important event from the book.

4. Gather three copies of template #2.

5. Label each copy of template #2 with "Beginning," "Middle," or "End." Then, write one or two sentences each about the beginning, middle, and end of the book on each template.

6. Draw and color a picture on each template to match what you wrote.

7. Cut out the pages and staple them together to form a book.

Notes to the Teacher:

- Assign students to small groups to read a book together.

- Make enough copies of Mini-Book Template #2 so that each group can complete its mini-book.

What You Need:

pencil

Mini-Book Templates

crayons, colored pencils, markers

scissors

stapler

Mini-Book Template #1

Title _____

_____

Author _____

Names _____

Mini-Book Template #2

Story House

What You Do:

1. Build a house to show the plot of a book you have read.

2. Write the book title and author's name on the roof of the house on the Story House Template.

3. Color and cut out the house.

4. Cut on the heavy black lines of the three windows and the garage door. Bend the cut pieces to form the window and garage door openings.

5. Glue the house to a sheet of light-colored construction paper. Make sure you do not glue the windows and garage door shut.

6. Write two sentences in each top window opening to tell about the beginning and middle of the book.

7. Write two sentences in the opening of the garage door to tell about the end of the book.

8. In the opening of the bottom window, write the main characters' names.

9. Write your name on the bottom of the construction paper.

What You Need:
pencil

Story House Template

crayons, colored pencils

scissors

12" x 18" light-colored construction paper

glue

Note to the Teacher:
Enlarge the template so that students have enough room to write in the window and door openings.

Story House Template

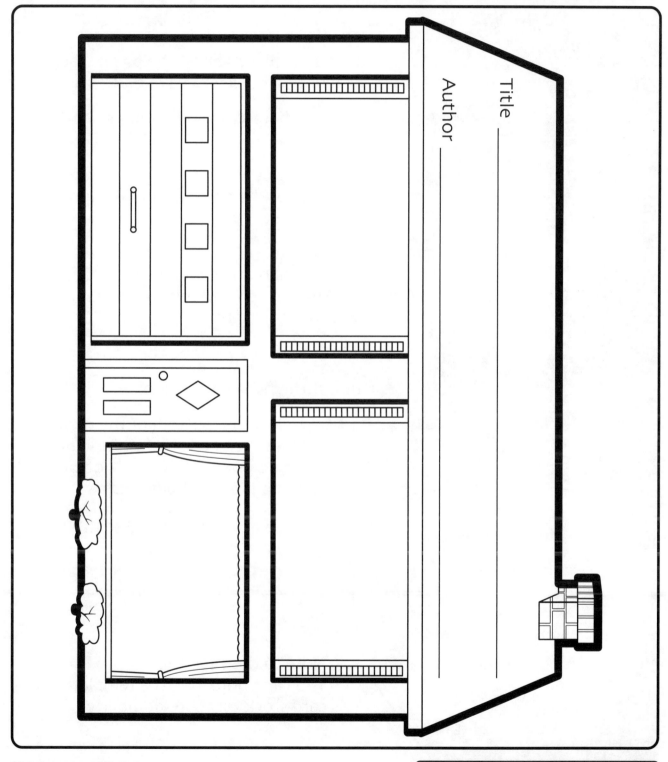

Title

Author

Fishing Mobile

What You Do:

1. Make a fishing mobile to help you "catch" the plot of a book you have read.

2. Write the book title and author's name on the hook on Fishing Mobile Template #1.

3. Write two or three sentences about the beginning of the book on the "Beginning" fish.

4. On template #2, write two or three sentences about the middle of the book on the "Middle" fish and two or three sentences about the end of the book on the "End" fish.

5. Lightly color the fish and the hook.

6. Cut out the fish and the hook.

7. Punch a hole in the bottom of the hook (where shown) and the top of the "End" fish. Punch holes in the top and bottom of the "Beginning" and "Middle" fish.

8. Use yarn to tie the three fish to the hook in order. If you need help tying the yarn, ask your teacher.

9. Write your name on the back of the hook.

Note to the Teacher:
You can photocopy the templates on card stock for more durability.

What You Need:

Fishing Mobile Templates

pencil

crayons, colored pencils

scissors

hole punch

3 pieces of yarn

Fishing Mobile Template #1

Title

Author

Beginning

Fishing Mobile Template #2

Middle

_____

_____

_____

_____

End

_____

_____

_____

_____

Book Box

What You Do:

1. Show off the characters, setting, and scenes from a book you have read by making a book box.

2. Cover an empty square tissue box (including the bottom) with contact paper or white construction paper. Use glue or tape to attach the paper to the box.

3. Turn the box upside down and write the book title, author's name, and your name.

4. On each side of the box, draw and color a picture of a character, the setting, or a scene from the book.

5. Show your book box to the class and explain how each picture you drew matches something from the book.

What You Need:

empty square tissue box

white construction paper or contact paper

scissors

glue or tape

markers, crayons

BOOK LEAF

What You Do:

1. Add a leaf to your class book tree after you have read a book.

2. Write the book title and author's name on the Book Leaf Template.

3. Write one or two sentences about why you liked the book. You can include information about the characters, setting, or plot.

4. Lightly color the leaf and cut it out.

5. Write your name on the back of the leaf.

6. Use tape or glue to attach your leaf to the class book tree.

Notes to the Teacher:

- You can copy the template on card stock for more durability.

- Use butcher paper to make a large tree on a wall or bulletin board.

What You Need:

pencil

Book Leaf Template

colored pencils

scissors

tape or glue

Book Leaf Template

Title _____

_____

_____

Author_____

_____

I like this book because _____

_____

_____

_____

*Author *Bouquet*

What You need:

pencil

Author Bouquet Templates

crayons, colored pencils

scissors

glue or stapler

What You Do:

1. Make a flower bouquet for the author of several books your group has read.

2. Choose a book from the basket and write the book title and two or three sentences that tell about the book on Author Bouquet Template #1.

3. Lightly color your petal and cut it out.

4. Gather your group's petals and work as a group to make the rest of the flower.

5. Write the author's name in the circle on template #2.

6. Cut out the circle. Glue or staple the petals around it.

7. Write your name and the names of the classmates in your group on the leaves on template #3. Cut out the leaves and stem.

8. Glue or staple the stem to the rest of the flower.

Notes to the Teacher:

- Assign students to small groups to read books together. Give each group a basket of books written by the same author.

- Each student should pick at least one book and make a flower petal for it.

Author Bouquet Template #1

Title _____

_____

Summary _____

_____

_____

_____

Author Bouquet Template #2

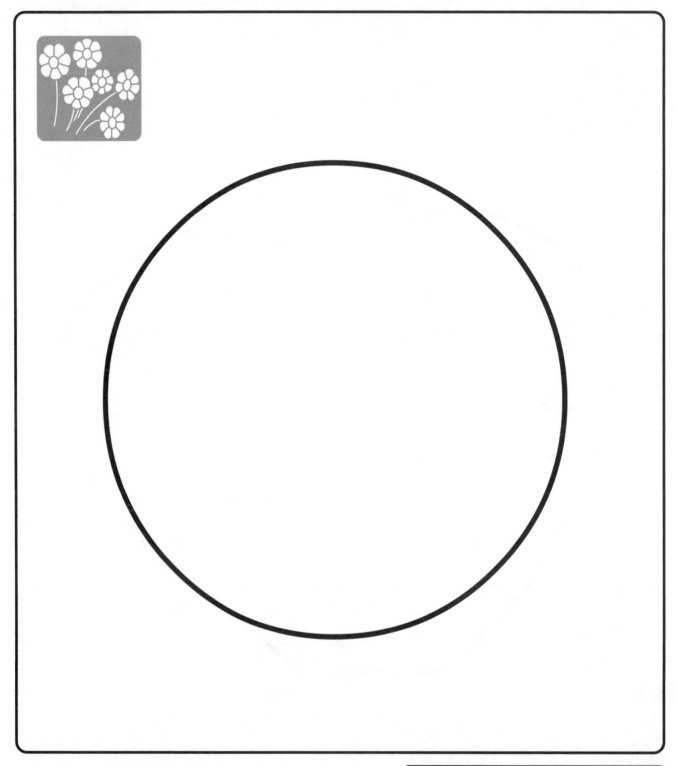

Author Bouquet Template #3

ABC Class Book

What You Do:

1. Make an ABC book about a topic your class has studied or a book you have read.

2. As a class, brainstorm ideas about the topic or book that match each letter of the alphabet.

   For example, you might use the following for a science unit about reptiles:

   A is for alligator.
   B is for burrow.

3. Color and cut out your letter from the ABC Class Book Template.

4. Glue your letter beside the line on the activity sheet. Then, on the line write the word that corresponds with the letter.

5. Draw and color a matching picture under the word. Write your name on the bottom of the page.

Notes to the Teacher:

- This activity can be completed with various topics, including science and social studies units.

- After the class has brainstormed ideas, assign each student a letter of the alphabet.

- Create a cover for the students' pictures or have students work together to make one out of construction paper. Bind the cover and activity sheets together to create a class book.

What You Need:

ABC Class Book Template

crayons, markers, colored pencils

scissors

glue

ABC Class Book Activity Sheet

pencil

construction paper (optional)

ABC Class Book Template

A B
C D E F G H
I J K L M N
O P Q R S T
U V W X Y Z

ABC Class Book Activity Sheet

is for

_____

Name _____